D1231194

Birthday Cakes for Kids

Publications International, Ltd.
Favorite Brand Name Recipes at www.fbnr.com

Giant Gift Boxes

1 package (18¼ ounces) chocolate or vanilla cake mix,
   plus ingredients to prepare mix
1 container (16 ounces) white frosting
   Orange and neon green food coloring
   Yellow tube icing
   Assorted decors and sprinkles
   Candles (optional)

1. Prepare and bake cake mix according to package directions for two 8- or 9-inch square cakes. Cool cakes completely before frosting. Combine half container of frosting and orange food coloring in medium bowl; mix until desired shade is reached. Repeat with remaining frosting and green food coloring.

2. Place one cake layer on serving plate. Frost top and sides with green frosting. Squeeze icing onto cake to resemble ribbon. Place second cake layer at angle to first cake layer as shown in photo. Frost top and sides with orange frosting. Squeeze icing on cake top and sides to resemble ribbons. Decorate with additional icing and decors as desired. Place candles in cake, if desired.

Makes 12 servings

Birthday Cakes
for Kids

4

Kitty Kat

1 package (18¼ ounces) carrot cake mix with pudding in
    the mix, plus ingredients to prepare mix
1 container (16 ounces) cream cheese frosting
   Red and yellow food coloring
¼ cup chocolate sprinkles
1 red heart-shaped candy or gumdrop
2 black round candies or black licorice gumdrops
   Black licorice strip
2 homemade or purchased cupcakes
   Candles or pieces uncooked spaghetti

1. Prepare and bake cake mix according to package directions
for two 8- or 9-inch round cakes. Cool cakes completely before
frosting. Combine frosting and food coloring in medium bowl; mix
until desired shade of orange is reached.

2. Place one cake layer on serving plate. Frost top of cake. Place
second cake layer on top. Frost top and side of cake. Cut ⅜-inch
from 3 sides of each cupcakes to make triangles. Position triangles
on cake for ears; frost. Make fur on cake using tines of fork. Scatter
sprinkles around top edge of cake.

3. Place red candy for nose and round candies for eyes. Cut
licorice strips into 3½-inch lengths; place on cake for mouth as
shown in photo. Place candles for whiskers as shown in photo.

Makes 12 servings

Birthday Cakes
for Kids

5

Mad Hatter

1 large (12-inch) flour tortilla
Nonstick cooking spray
1 package (18¼ ounces) cake mix (any flavor), plus
   ingredients to prepare mix
2 containers (16 ounces each) white frosting
Food coloring, any color
Assorted round citrus-flavored gummy candies
Candy-coated chocolate pieces
Wafer cookie

1. Preheat oven to 350°F. Spray both sides of tortilla lightly with cooking spray; place on baking sheet. Bake about 10 minutes or until lightly browned; allow to cool. Prepare and bake cake mix according to package directions for one 8-inch round cake and one 9-inch round cake. Cool cakes completely before frosting.

2. Combine frosting and food coloring in large bowl; mix until desired shade is reached. Gently spread thin layer of frosting on one side of tortilla. Place, frosted side up, on serving plate.

3. Center 8-inch cake layer on tortilla. Frost top and side. Top with 9-inch layer; frost top and side. Decorate cake with gummy candies and chocolate pieces as shown in photo or as desired. Decorate wafer cookie, if desired. Place against side of cake as shown in photo. *Makes 12 servings*

Coronation Cake

2 packages (18¼ ounces each) white cake mix, plus
    ingredients to prepare mix
2 teaspoons orange extract
2 containers (18 ounces each) vanilla frosting
    Pink or red food coloring
1 to 1½ packages (7 ounces each) flaked coconut
1 purchased tiara

1. Preheat oven to 350°F. Cut parchment paper to fit bottoms of two 10-inch round cake pans. Spray with nonstick cooking spray. Prepare cake mixes according to package directions. Add orange extract to batter; mix well. Divide batter evenly between prepared pans. Bake 30 minutes or until toothpick inserted into centers comes out clean. Cool cakes completely before frosting.

2. Place one cake layer on serving plate. Combine frosting and food coloring in large bowl; mix until desired shade of pink is reached. Spread frosting over top of cake. Place second layer on top of frosting. Frost top and side of cake.

3. Gently press coconut onto side of cake. Place tiara in center of cake.
Makes 24 servings

Birthday Cakes
for Kids

Swiss Dotted Tiered Birthday Cake

2 packages (18¼ ounces each) white cake mix, plus ingredients to prepare mix
Grated peel of 3 lemons
2 containers (16 ounces each) lemon frosting
Pastel-colored candy-coated fruit candies

1. Preheat oven to 350°F. Cut parchment paper to fit bottom of one 6-inch, one 8-inch and one 10-inch round cake pan. Spray cake pans with nonstick cooking spray.

2. Prepare cake mix according to package directions. Add lemon peel to batter; mix well. Place about 1¾ cups batter into 6-inch pan, about 2¾ cups batter into 8-inch pan and about 4¼ cups batter into 10-inch pan. Bake 10-inch cake 28 to 30 minutes and 6-inch and 8-inch cakes 33 to 35 minutes or until toothpick inserted into centers comes out clean. Cool cakes completely before frosting.

3. Place 10-inch cake layer upside down on serving plate. Frost top and side of cake. If 8-inch cake top is rounded, cut off top with long serrated knife. Place, flat side down, centered on 10-inch cake layer. Frost top and side of cake. If 6-inch top is rounded, cut off top with long serrated knife. Place, flat side down, centered on 8-inch cake layer. Frost top and side of 6-inch cake. Decorate with candies.

Makes 24 servings

Birthday Cakes for Kids

8

Toy Jeep

- **1 container (16 ounces) white frosting, divided**
- **¼ cup prepared chocolate frosting**
- **Food coloring, any two colors**
- **1 frozen pound cake (10 ounces), thawed**
- **2 individual sponge cakes with cream filling**
- **½ graham cracker**
- **4 chocolate frosted mini doughnuts**
- **2 red gumdrops**
- **2 yellow gumdrops**
- **Black licorice strings**
- **2 pretzel rods or pieces chocolate licorice**

1. Combine all but ½ cup white frosting and one color food coloring in large bowl; mix until desired shade is reached. Place pound cake on serving plate; frost top and sides of cake with frosting. Combine ¼ cup white frosting and chocolate frosting in small bowl; mix well. Place sponge cakes, flat side forward, on center and back of cake to make seats; frost with light brown frosting. Cut small slit in front of car. Slide graham cracker half into slit. Combine remaining ¼ cup frosting and remaining color food coloring in small bowl; mix until desired shade is reached; frost graham cracker.

2. Press doughnuts onto sides of cake as wheels. Decorate as desired. Place red gumdrops as rear lights and yellow candies on front for headlights. Bend licorice and place on top of seats. Cut pretzels as needed and press onto front as bumper.   *Makes 10 servings*

Birthday Cakes
for Kids

9

Magical Castle

1 package (18¼ ounces) yellow cake mix, plus
    ingredients to prepare mix
2 containers (16 ounce each) white frosting
    Blue food coloring
4 sugar ice cream cones
4 individual sponge cakes with cream filling
1 flat-bottomed ice cream cone
8 wafer cookies
    Assorted gumdrops and small candies
    Colored licorice strips

1. Prepare and bake cake mix according to package directions for two 8- or 9-inch square cakes. Cool cakes completely before frosting.

2. Combine frosting and food coloring in large bowl; mix until desired shade is reached. Place one cake layer on serving platter; frost top. Top with second cake layer; frost top and sides of cake.

3. Place one sugar cone on top of each sponge cake, pushing cake gently halfway into cone. Frost cones and sponge cakes; press each onto one corner of cake as shown in photo. Decorate tops of cones as desired. Frost flat-bottomed cone; place in center of cake. Press two wafer cookies onto center of each side of cake as castle doors. Decorate cake as desired with assorted gumdrops and small candies. Place licorice strips to form path into castle.   *Makes 16 servings*

Figure 8 Race Track

   1 package (18¼ ounces) chocolate cake mix, plus
       ingredients to prepare mix
1½ cups shredded coconut
     Green food coloring
   1 container (16 ounces) chocolate frosting
     White candy coated licorice bits
     Candy rocks (optional)

1. Prepare and bake cake mix according to package directions for two 8- or 9-inch round cake pans. Cool completely before frosting.

2. Combine coconut and 4 to 5 drops food coloring in resealable food storage bag; seal bag. Shake bag until coconut is evenly tinted.

3. Place cake layers, side by side on large serving platter. Frost tops and sides of cakes. Using small bowl or cup as guide, trace 2½-inch circle in center of each cake with knife tip. Sprinkle inside of each circle with small amount of coconut. Press remaining coconut onto cake sides, allowing to come up over cake edge.

4. Draw figure-eight pattern into frosting using fork. Place licorice bits around centers of cakes to make lanes. Decorate with candy rocks, toy cars and flags, if desired. *Makes 12 servings*

Flutter Away

1 package (18¼ ounces) white or chocolate cake mix,
    plus ingredients to prepare mix
1 container (16 ounces) vanilla frosting
    Food coloring, any color(s)
1 pirouette cookie, any flavor
    Gumdrops, gummy hearts and small round candies

1. Preheat oven to 350°F. Grease and flour two 9-inch round cake pans. Prepare cake mix according to package directions. Bake cakes 28 to 31 minutes or until toothpick inserted into centers comes out clean. Cool completely before frosting. Combine frosting and food coloring in medium bowl; mix until desired shade is reached.

2. Cut each cake layer crosswise in half. Place two halves on serving plate, cut sides facing out; frost top of cakes. Top each half with remaining halves. Using serrated knife, cut triangles two-thirds down from top of each half to form butterfly wings as shown in photo.

3. Frost top and sides of cake with remaining frosting. Place cookie between cake halves to form butterfly body. Decorate wings with candies as desired. *Makes 12 servings*

Birthday Cakes
for Kids
12

Big Rig
Logging Truck

1 frozen pound cake (16 ounces), thawed
1 container (16 ounces) chocolate frosting
1 frozen pound cake (10 ounces), thawed
8 chocolate sandwich cookies
8 small red candies
15 large (8-inch) pretzel rods
4 large red gumdrops
2 large yellow gumdrops
  Silver dragées (optional)
1 (7 to 8-inch) candle

1. Place 16-ounce pound cake on serving platter; frost top and sides of cake. Cut 3-inch slice from one end of 10-ounce pound cake and place on one end of frosted cake to resemble truck cab; frost top and sides. (Reserve remaining portion of 10-ounce pound cake for another use.)

2. Place small amount of frosting onto center of each sandwich cookie. Press one red candy onto each cookie; push cookies onto sides of cake to resemble wheels.as shown in photo.

3. Break 2 pretzel rods in half and push vertically into cake at sides as shown in photo. Lay remaining pretzel rods on top of cake. Push 2 red gumdrops onto back of cake to resemble tail lights and remaining 2 red gumdrops on top of cab. Push 2 yellow gumdrops onto truck front to resemble headlights.

4. Press dragées onto cake as shown in photo, if desired. Push candle into side of cake.   *Makes 12 servings*

Birthday Cakes
for Kids

Colossal Birthday Cupcake

1 package (18¼ ounces) devil's food cake mix, plus ingredients to prepare mix
2 containers (18 ounces each) vanilla or chocolate frosting, divided
¼ cup creamy peanut butter
Construction paper or aluminum foil
Fruit-flavored candy wafers or chocolate shavings
Candle (optional)

1. Preheat oven to 350°F. Grease and flour two 8-inch round cake pans. Prepare cake mix according to package directions. Bake about 30 minutes or until toothpick inserted into centers comes out clean. Cool completely before frosting.

2. Place one cake layer on serving plate. Combine ¾ cup frosting and peanut butter in medium bowl. Spread frosting mixture over top of cake. Top with second cake layer. Frost top of cake with remaining frosting. Mound frosting slightly higher in center.

3. Cut paper into 36×3½-inch piece. Pleat paper every ½ inch. Wrap around side of cake. Place candy wafers decoratively on frosting. Place one candle in center of cake, if desired.

Makes 12 servings

Birthday Cakes for Kids

14

Happy Clown Face

1 package (18¼ ounces) yellow cake mix, plus
    ingredients to prepare mix
1 container (16 ounces) white frosting
    Food coloring, any color
    Assorted gumdrops, gummy, candies, colored licorice
    strings and other candies
1 party hat
    Candles

1. Prepare and bake cake according to package directions for two
8- or 9-inch round cakes. Cool cakes completely before frosting.

2. Combine frosting and food coloring in large bowl; mix until
desired shade is reached. Place one cake layer on serving plate.
Frost top of cake. Place second cake layer on top; frost top and side
of cake. Decorate face of clown using assorted candies as desired.
Place party hat and candles on cake as shown in photo or as
desired. *Makes 12 servings*

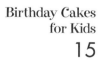

Birthday Cakes
for Kids

Jack in the Box

1 package (18¼ ounces) cake mix (any flavor), plus
    ingredients to prepare mix
1 scoop ice cream or sherbet, any flavor
  Assorted candies
  Food coloring, any colors
1 container (16 ounces) white frosting
  Flat red candy strips or fruit leather
1 sugar ice cream cone

1. Prepare and bake cake mix according package directions for two 8- or 9-inch square cakes. Cool completely before frosting.

2. Place ice cream scoop in small dish. Decorate with candies to resemble face. Place in freezer until serving time.

3. Divide and tint frosting as desired. Cut one cake into 4 equal pieces. (Reserve remaining cake for another use.) Place one piece on serving plate; frost top. Repeat with three other pieces. Frost top and sides of entire cake. Press desired candies around top, base and edges of cake. Decorate with additional candies, if desired.

4. Create clown collar by pinching remaining candy strips into 4-inch circle and center on cake top. Decorate sugar cone, if desired. When ready to serve, center decorated ice scream scoop on cake and top with ice cream cone. Serve immediately.

Makes 6 servings

Ladybug

1 package (18¼ ounces) white cake mix, plus ingredients
    to prepare mix
1 container (16 ounces) vanilla frosting
¼ cup red raspberry jam
    Red colored sugar
    Miniature brown candy-coated chocolate pieces
8 dark chocolate discs or mint chocolate cookies
    Large mint candy patty
    String licorice and assorted gumdrops
1 cup sweetened shredded coconut
    Green food coloring

1. Prepare and bake cake mix according to package directions for two 9-inch round cakes. Cool completely before frosting. Place one cake layer on serving plate. Frost top with vanilla frosting. Spread raspberry preserves within ½ inch from edge. Top with second cake layer. Frost top and side with remaining frosting.

2. Sprinkle top of cake with red sugar. Create wings of ladybug with chocolate pieces as shown in photo. Place chocolate discs on top of cake for ladybug spots. Using string licorice and assorted gumdrops create ladybug face. Attach to mint patty using small amounts of frosting. Place mint patty on cake.

3. Combine coconut and 8 to 10 drops food coloring in resealable plastic food storage bag; seal bag. Shake bag until color is evenly distributed. Press tinted coconut on side of cake. Decorate edge of cake as desired.
Makes 12 servings

Birthday Cakes
for Kids

Big Purple Purse

1 package (18¼ ounces) cake mix (any flavor), plus
    ingredients to prepare mix
1 container (16 ounces) white frosting
    Blue and red food coloring
1 piece red licorice rope
1 white chocolate-coated pretzel
    Round sugar-coated colored candies
    Candy lipstick, necklace and ring (optional)

1. Preheat oven to 350°F. Prepare and bake cake mix according to package directions for two 9-inch round cake pans. Cool cakes completely before frosting. Reserve one cake layer for another use.

2. Combine frosting and food coloring in medium bowl. Mix until desired shade of purple is reached.

3. Spread about ½ cup frosting over top of cake layer. Cut cake in half; press frosted sides together to form half circle. Place cake, cut sides down, on serving plate.

4. Spread frosting over top and sides of cake. Cut licorice rope in half; press ends into top of cake to form purse handle. Add pretzel for clasp. Gently press round candies into sides of cake. Arrange candy lipstick, necklace and ring around cake, if desired.

Makes 8 to 10 servings

Olympic Gold Cake

1 package (18¼ ounces) banana cake mix with pudding
    in the mix, plus ingredients to prepare mix
2 containers (18 ounces) cream cheese frosting
    Blue food coloring
2 cups chopped nuts, toasted
    Tube frosting in Olympic rings colors
⅔ cup semisweet chocolate chips, melted

1. Preheat oven to 350°F. Grease and flour two 9-inch round cake pans. Prepare cake mix according to package directions. Bake 22 minutes or until toothpick inserted into centers comes out clean. Cool completely before frosting.

2. Combine frosting and food coloring in large bowl; mix until desired shade is reached. Place one cake layer on serving plate. Spread ¾ cup frosting over top of cake. Top with second cake layer. Frost top and side of cake with remaining frosting. Gently press nuts onto side of cake.

3. Pipe five Olympic rings using tube frosting as shown in photo. Place melted chocolate in small resealable food storage bag; seal bag. Cut off very small corner from bag. Pipe "Olympic Gold" or desired words on cake. *Makes 12 servings*

Tip: To easily make Olympic rings, turn a 2-inch-wide round juice cup upside down and press into frosting five times in desired location. This will act as a stencil to make perfect rings.

Birthday Cakes
for Kids

19

Flower Power

**1 package (18¼ ounces) spice cake mix, plus ingredients
    to prepare mix
1 container (16 ounces) white frosting
    Food coloring, any color(s)
5 to 10 large marshmallows
1 cup multi-colored miniature marshmallows
    Decorating sugar, any color**

1. Prepare and bake cake mix according to package directions for two 8- or 9-inch round cake pans. Cool completely before frosting.

2. Combine frosting and food coloring in large bowl; mix until desired shade is reached. Place one cake layer on serving plate; frost top of cake. Top with second cake layer. Frost top and side of cake.

3. Cut each marshmallow cross-wise into 3 pieces using clean scissors. Place five marshmallow pieces in circular pattern, pressing lightly into frosting. Repeat until cake has desired amount of evenly spaced flowers. Press miniature marshmallows around cake base as shown in photo. Sprinkle center of each flower with sugar.

Makes 12 servings

Slam Dunk

1 package (18¼ ounces) dark chocolate cake mix, plus
   ingredients to prepare mix
¾ cup crushed chocolate sandwich cookies (8 to 10)
1 container (16 ounces) dark chocolate frosting
1 cup prepared vanilla frosting
   Red, yellow and blue food coloring
   Brown mini candy-coated chocolate pieces
   Orange candy-coated chocolate pieces

1. Preheat oven to 350°F. Grease and flour two 9-inch round cake pans. Prepare cake mix according to package directions. Bake 30 to 33 minutes or until toothpick inserted into centers comes out clean. Cool completely before frosting.

2. Place one cake layer on serving plate; spread with chocolate frosting. Sprinkle crushed cookie crumbs over frosting. Top with second cake layer. Frost side of cake with chocolate frosting being careful not to get frosting on top of cake.

3. Combine vanilla frosting and few drops of red, yellow and blue food coloring in small bowl until desired shade of orange is reached. Spread on top of cake. Using meat mallet, gently press into frosting to create texture of basketball. Create basketball lines on top of cake using mini chocolate pieces. Press orange chocolate pieces around bottom of cake as shown in photo. *Makes 12 servings*

Birthday Cakes
for Kids

Teddy Bear

1 package (18¼ ounces) chocolate cake mix, plus
    ingredients to prepare mix
1 container (16 ounces) chocolate frosting
4 homemade or purchased cupcakes
1 package (12 ounce) semisweet mini chocolate chips
2 large white gumdrops or mini cookies
2 small black round gummy candies
¼ cup butterscotch or peanut butter chips
2 heart-shaped gummy candies *or* ¼ cup white chocolate
    chips
1 red gumdrop or small round gummy candy
    Black and red licorice strips

1. Prepare and bake cake mix according to package directions for two 8- or 9-inch round cakes. Cool cakes completely before frosting. Place one cake layer on serving platter and frost top. Top with second layer and frost top and side. Stack two cupcakes and frost; repeat with remaining cupcakes. Position each stack at top of cake to resemble ears, as shown in photo. Place heart gummy candies on ears. Press semisweet chips around side and top edge of cake and ears.

2. Flatten two white gumdrops with rolling pin. Place on cake as eyes. Attach black gumdrops with small amount of frosting to white gumdrops as shown in photo. Make 2-inch mound of butterscotch chips for snout. Place red gumdrop in center of butterscotch chips for nose. Cut black and red licorice strips to create mouth and eyebrows as shown in photo. *Makes 16 servings*

Sherbet Starburst

**1 package (18¼ ounces) lemon cake mix, plus
    ingredients to prepare mix**
**2 quarts raspberry or mango sherbet, or flavors of choice
    Yellow food coloring**
**2 containers (15 ounces each) white pourable frosting
    Orange decorating sugar**

1. Prepare and bake cake according to package directions for two 8- or 9-inch round cakes. Cool cakes completely before frosting.

2. Scoop sherbet into well rounded balls; place in small dish. Freeze until ready to serve.

3. Combine frosting and food coloring in large microwavable bowl; mix until desired shade is reached. Cut one cake layer into 8 wedges. (Reserve remaining cake layer for another use.) Place cake on wire rack over baking sheet to catch drips. Microwave frosting on HIGH 20 seconds; stir well. Pour frosting slowly over each cake wedge, makings sure to cover all sides. Sprinkle with sugar sprinkles. Allow cake pieces to sit until frosting becomes firm, about 20 minutes.

4. At serving time, arrange cakes pieces in a circle with tips pointing out as shown in photo. Place dish of sherbet in center of cake pieces.   *Makes 8 servings*

Birthday Cakes
for Kids

Time to Party

1 package (18¼ ounces) carrot cake mix with pudding in the mix, plus ingredients to prepare mix
2 containers (16 ounces each) cream cheese frosting
Food coloring, any color
12 chocolate candy discs
Candy-coated chocolate and peanut pieces
Tube icings
Wax letter candles (optional)

1. Preheat oven to 350°F. Grease two 9-inch round cake pans. Prepare cake mix according to package directions. Bake about 22 minutes or until toothpick inserted into centers comes out clean. Cool completely before frosting.

2. Combine frosting and food coloring in large bowl; mix until desired shade is reached. Place one cake layer on serving plate. Spread ¾ cup frosting over top of cake. Top with second cake layer. Frost top and side of cake with remaining frosting.

3. Place chocolate candies in position of clock numbers on cake. Pipe numbers onto face of each chocolate candy using icing.

4. Make hands of clock using chocolate and peanut pieces. Place at desired time. Press remaining chocolate pieces around cake base as shown in photo, if desired. Spell out "Time to Party" on cake using wax candles, if desired.   *Makes 12 servings*

Birthday Cakes
for Kids

24

Beautiful Butterflies

1 package (18¼ ounces) spice cake mix with pudding in
    the mix, plus ingredients to prepare mix
2 containers (16 ounces each) cream cheese or white
    chocolate frosting
  Food coloring, any color
8 to 10 round chocolate wafer cookies, cut in half
  Pastel-colored candy-coated chocolate pieces
  Colored decorating sugar (optional)
  Confetti sprinkles (optional)

1. Preheat oven to 350°F. Grease and flour two 8-inch round cake pans. Prepare cake mix according to package instructions. Bake 30 minutes or until toothpick inserted into centers comes out clean. Cool completely before frosting.

2. Combine frosting and food coloring in large bowl; mix until desired shade is reached. Place one cake layer on cake plate. Spread ½ cup frosting over top of cake. Place second cake layer over frosting. Frost top and side of cake.

3. Place two wafer halves about ½ inch apart, cut sides facing outward. Repeat with remaining wafer halves around cake. Place two chocolate pieces in between two wafer cookies as shown in photo. Use remaining pieces to decorate cake as desired. Sprinkle colored sugar over cake, if desired. Make antennas using sprinkles, if desired. *Makes 12 servings*

Candy Cottage

1 package (18¼ ounces) cake mix (any flavor), plus
    ingredients to prepare mix
1 container (16 ounces) white frosting
    Food coloring, any color(s)
1 cup round gummy candies
1 graham cracker
4 strawberry-flavored wafer cookies
    Small assorted round candies
    Sugar-coated green candy straws or strips
    Colored licorice strips

1. Prepare and bake cake mix according to package directions for 13×9-inch cake. Cool cake completely before frosting.

2. Combine frosting and food coloring in large bowl; mix until desired shade is reached. Place cake on serving platter; frost top and sides.

3. Draw outline of roof shape with toothpick or knife. Fill roof with round gummy candies. Place one graham cracker on cake to resemble door where desired, trimming if necessary. Place two wafer cookies to resemble shutters on either side of door. Use green candy strips to create foliage and assorted candies as flowers around base of cottage. Attach additional candies with frosting resemble door knob and shutter decorations. Outline roof, door and windows with licorice strips, if desired. *Makes 12 servings*

Flag Birthday Cake

1 package (18¼ ounces) devil's food cake mix, plus
    ingredients to prepare mix
1 package (about 11 ounces) peanut butter and
    chocolate chips
2 containers (16 ounces each) milk chocolate frosting
   Assorted fruit leathers
   Candles or thin pretzel sticks

1. Preheat oven to 350°F. Grease and flour two 8-inch round cake pans. Prepare cake mix according to package directions. Add ⅓ cup peanut butter and chocolate chips to batter. Divide batter evenly between prepared pans. Bake 30 minutes or until toothpick inserted into centers comes out clean. Cool completely before frosting.

2. Place one cake layer on serving plate. Spread ½ cup frosting over top of cake. Top with second cake layer. Frost top and side of cake with remaining frosting. Gently press remaining peanut butter and chocolate chips onto side and outer edge of cake top.

3. To make flags, cut desired amount of triangles out of fruit leathers. Make two ½- to ¾-inch horizontal cuts along short side of one triangle. Weave one candle in and out of cuts. Repeat with remaining triangles and candies. Place flags around cake.

Makes 12 servings

Note: Flags can be decorated with the birthday child's name or the name of each guest attending the party.

Birthday Cakes
for Kids

27

Giant Hot Dog

1 frozen pound cake (16 ounces), thawed
½ container (16 ounces) chocolate frosting
3 individual sponge cakes with cream filling
   Yellow tube icing
   Green gumdrops, diced

1. Cut ½-inch triangles off corners of pound cake. (Save triangles for another use, if desired.) Cut cake horizontally in half, cutting almost all the way through, but leaving cake halves attached. Place sliced cake on serving plate to resemble bun.

2. Cut ¼-inch off both ends of one sponge cake; place in center of bun. Cut one end off remaining sponge cakes. Place, cut ends together, on either side of first sponge cake to resemble hot dog.

3. Spread frosting on hot dog, being careful to avoid bun. Squeeze yellow icing on hot dog to resemble mustard. Sprinkle diced gumdrops on hot dog to resemble relish.   *Makes 12 servings*

Birthday Cakes
for Kids

28

Dolphin Cake

2 packages (18¼ ounces each) orange cake mix, plus ingredients to prepare mix
2 containers (16 ounces each) vanilla frosting
Green and blue food coloring
Blue mini candy-coated chocolate pieces
Silver dragées (optional)
Blue decorating sugar (optional)
Blue rock candy (optional)

1. Preheat oven to 350°F. Grease 13×9-inch baking pan. Prepare cake mixes according to package directions. Pour all but 2 cups batter into prepared pan. (Reserve remaining batter for another use.) Bake 35 minutes or until toothpick inserted into center comes out clean. Cool completely before frosting.

2. Reserve ¼ cup frosting. Combine remaining frosting and green food coloring in large bowl; mix until desired shade is reached. Place cake on serving plate; frost top and sides. Draw outline of dolphin in center of cake using wooden toothpick. Combine reserved ¼ cup frosting and blue food coloring in small bowl; mix until desired shade is reached. Spread thin layer of blue frosting in outline. Decorate dolphin with chocolate pieces, dragées and sugar, if desired. Decorate bottom and sides of cake as desired.

Makes 20 servings

Birthday Cakes
for Kids

29

Lollipop Garden Bouquet

1 package (18¼ ounces) carrot cake mix, plus ingredients
  to prepare mix
1 container (16 ounces) white frosting
  Green food coloring
½ cup crushed chocolate wafer cookies
  Round hard sweet and sour candies
20 hard candy rings
  Green fruit leather
6 to 10 lollipops

1. Prepare and bake cake mix according to package directions
for one 8-inch round cake and one 9-inch round cake. Cool cakes
completely before frosting. Combine frosting and food coloring in
medium bowl; mix until desired shade is reached. Place 8-inch cake
layer on serving plate. Frost top and cover with 9-inch cake layer.
Frost top and sides of cakes.

2. Sprinkle cookie crumbs over top of cake leaving ½-inch border
without crumbs. Press sweet and sour candies around cake top as
shown in photo. Decorate 8-inch cake layer with candy rings.

3. Using scissors, cut fruit leather into 2½-inch leaf shapes and
press onto lollipop sticks. Push lollipops into cake center.

Makes 12 servings

Moonscape

1 package (18¼ ounces) chocolate cake mix, plus
    ingredients to prepare mix
1 container (16 ounces) white frosting
2 cups large marshmallows
2 cups mini marshmallows
¼ cup powdered sugar
    Alien toys, spacecraft, flag (optional)

1. Prepare and bake cake according to package directions for
13×9-inch cake baked in a metal pan. Cool cake completely
before frosting.

2. Preheat broiler. Spread thin layer of frosting over cake. Sprinkle
all marshmallows over frosting as shown in photo or as desired.
Place cake under broiler 30 seconds or until marshmallows begin to
brown. (Watch carefully to avoid burning.) Sprinkle with powdered
sugar. Decorate cake with toys, if desired.   *Makes 12 servings*

Birthday Cakes
for Kids

Pink Piggy

1 package (18¼ ounces) white cake mix, plus ingredients
   to prepare mix
1 container (16 ounces) white frosting
   Pink or red food coloring
3 homemade or purchased cupcakes
   Pink decorating sugar
4 small round gummy candies (about ¼ inch in diameter)
   or black jelly beans
   Black decorating icing or licorice strings
2 feet curly ribbon (optional)

1. Prepare and bake cake mix according to package directions for
two 8- or 9-inch round cakes. Cool cakes completely before frosting.
Combine frosting and food coloring in medium bowl; mix until
desired shade is reached. Place one cake layer on serving platter;
frost entire cake. (Reserve remaining cake layer for another use.)

2. Cut ⅜ inch from 3 sides of 2 cupcakes to create triangles.
Position ears on side of cake; cover with frosting. Cut remaining
cupcake in half horizontally. Place cupcake half slightly below
center of cake; cover with frosting.

3. Sprinkle decorating sugar on cake as shown in photo. Press 2
gummy candies above snout for eyes and remaining 2 candies on
snout. Pipe icing above eyes to resemble lashes. Place ribbon as
shown in photo, if desired.   *Makes 6 servings*

Birthday Cakes
for Kids

32

Lollipop Flower Cake

1 package (18¼ ounces) French vanilla cake mix with pudding in the mix
1 cup milk
½ cup (1 stick) unsalted butter, softened
4 eggs
½ cup prepared lemon frosting
¼ cup whipping cream
    Food coloring, any color (optional)
    Toasted flaked coconut (optional)
½ small orange
    Decorated or plain lollipops

1. Preheat oven to 350°F. Spray 10-inch (12-cup) bundt pan with nonstick cooking spray.

2. Prepare cake mix according to package directions using 1 cup milk, ½ cup butter and 4 eggs in place of ingredients called for in package directions. (Batter will be thick.) Pour 5 cups batter into prepared pan. (Reserve remaining batter for another use.) Bake 35 minutes or until toothpick inserted near center comes out clean. Cool cake completely before frosting. Transfer to serving platter.

3. Combine frosting, cream and food coloring, if desired, in medium bowl. Mix until desired shade is reached. Spoon over top of cake, letting excess drip down side of cake. Sprinkle top of cake with coconut, if desired. Place orange half, cut side up, in center of cake to fill hole. Stick lollipops upright into orange.   *Makes 10 servings*

Pretty Princess Cake

1 package (18¼ ounces) cake mix (any flavor), plus
   ingredients to prepare mix
1 (8-inch) washable doll or doll cake pick
   Fruit leather, any color
8 to 10 large marshmallows
1 container (16 ounces) white frosting
   Food coloring, any color(s)
   Assorted candies

1. Prepare and bake cake according to package directions for
12-cup bundt pan. Cool completely before frosting. Wrap doll
torso and body with fruit leather to resemble clothing; set aside.

2. Place cake on serving platter. Push about 4 marshmallows into
cake center and insert doll. Continue adding marshmallows around
doll, until center is filled and doll is stable.

3. Combine frosting and food coloring in medium bowl; mix
until desired shade is reached. Frost top and side of cake. Make
decorative swirls in frosting as shown in photo, if desired. Decorate
cake with assorted candies as desired. *Makes 12 servings*

Rainbow Cake

**1 package (18 ounces) cake mix (any flavor), plus
     ingredients to prepare mix**
⅓ cup red raspberry jam
**1 container (16 ounces) vanilla frosting
     Rainbow-colored candy-coated fruit candies (at least
     5 different colors)**

1. Prepare and bake cake mix for two 8-inch round cake pans
according to package directions. Cool completely before frosting.

2. Place one layer upside down on serving platter. Spread jam on
top. Add second cake layer upside down to make flat cake top.
Frost entire cake with vanilla frosting.

3. Place string in straight line across center of cake; lift string to
remove. Using line left by string as guide, position row of red
candies across cake and down side. Place row of orange candies
on both sides of red row. Repeat with remaining candies in order
of colors of the rainbow: yellow, green, violet. Add row of candies
around base of cake, alternating colors.   *Makes 12 servings*

Variation: This exceptionally easy cake leaves lots of room for
personal creativity. Instead of a rainbow, position the candies in
spokes like a color wheel or in diagonal stripes spaced an inch or
two apart. Or, simply sprinkle the top of the cake with candies for
a festive polka dot look.

Stack o' CD's

1 package (18¼ ounces) yellow cake mix, plus
  ingredients to prepare mix
1 container (16 ounces) white frosting
  Food coloring, any color(s)
  White decorating sugar
  Edible silver dragées (optional)
1 round black licorice wheel

1. Prepare and bake cake mix according to package directions for two 6- or 8-inch round cakes. Cool cakes completely before frosting. Combine frosting and food coloring in medium bowl; mix until desired shade is reached. Center one cake layer on serving platter; frost top and side. Place second cake layer on first, offset of center by 1 inch. Frost top and side.

2. Using tines of fork add circular grooves. Sprinkle cake with white decorating sugar. Sprinkle dragées over cakes, if desired. Place round black licorice piece in center of top cake.

Makes 12 servings

Birthday Cakes
for Kids

36

I LUV U Cake

1 package (18¼ ounces) marble cake mix, plus
    ingredients to prepare mix
2 containers (16 ounces each) vanilla frosting
    Food coloring, any color(s)
    Colored confetti sprinkles
    Colored licorice strings or tube icing
1 chocolate candy kiss
    Black licorice string, cut into 1-inch pieces
    Mini candy-coated chocolate pieces
    Candy letters or tube icing

1. Preheat oven to 350°F. Grease two 8-inch round cake pans. Prepare cake mix according to package directions. Bake 30 minutes or until toothpick inserted into centers comes out clean. Cool completely before frosting.

2. Place one cake layer onto serving plate. Combine frosting and food coloring in large bowl; mix until desired shade is reached. Spread ½ cup frosting over top of cake. Place second cake layer on top of frosting. Frost top and side of cake with remaining frosting. Press confetti sprinkles around side of cake.

3. Make eye shape using colored licorice string, candy kiss and black licorice strings as shown in photo. Write "LUV U" with chocolate pieces as shown in photo. Place candy letters on cake as shown in photo.

Makes 12 servings

Birthday Cakes
for Kids

37

The Sweet Express

2 packages (18¼ ounces each) marble cake mix, plus
   ingredients to prepare mix
2 containers (16 ounces each) vanilla frosting
   Blue decorating spray
   Aerosol decorating icing, any 3 colors
½ cup chopped nuts
7 mini chocolate sandwich cookies
   Sugar coated sour gummy strips, any colors
   Gummy candy rings
   Assorted sprinkles
   Mini candy-coated chocolate pieces

1. Prepare and bake cake mixes according to package directions for two 13×9-inch cakes. Cool completely before frosting. Place one cake on serving tray. Frost top with frosting. Top with second cake. Frost top and sides with remaining frosting.

2. Spray top third of cake with blue decorating spray to resemble clouds. Using toothpick, draw outline for train cars. Following outline, frost each train car with desired icing color. Sprinkle chopped nuts under train cars. Place sandwich cookies on train cars to resemble wheels. Cut two small pieces of gummy strips to resemble car connectors. Place between train cars.

3. Cut two squares out of gummy strips; place on train to resemble windows. Cut shapes out of fruit leather to resemble cowcatcher and smoke stack as shown in photo. Place gummy candy rings on cake to resemble smoke rings. Top two remaining train cars with with desired candies, as shown in photo. Decorate edge of cake with mini candy-coated chocolate pieces, if desired. *Makes 24 servings*

Movie Marquee

1 package (18¼ ounces) chocolate fudge cake mix, plus
   ingredients to prepare mix
1 container (16 ounces) white frosting
1 bag (13 ounces) chocolate candy kisses
   Happy Birthday candles
   Star-shaped gummy candies
   Star-shaped candies

1. Prepare and bake cake according to package directions for
13×9-inch cake. Cool completely before frosting.

2. Remove cake from pan or leave in pan. Frost top and sides of
cake. Place candy kisses around border of cake. Use candles and
candies to decorate cake as desired.   *Makes 12 servings*

Birthday Cakes
for Kids
39

Strawberry Heart Cake

2 packages (18¼ ounces each) white cake mix, plus ingredients to prepare mix
1 teaspoons almond extract
2 teaspoons vanilla
2 containers (16 ounces each) buttercream-flavored frosting
Red food coloring
12 to 14 whole strawberries, cut in half through stem end

1. Preheat oven to 350°F. Cut parchment paper to fit bottom of 12×2-inch heart-shaped cake pan. Spray with nonstick cooking spray. Prepare cake mixes according to package directions. Add almond extract and vanilla; mix well. Pour 7½ cups batter into prepared pan; smooth to edges. (Reserve remaining batter for another use.) Bake about 40 minutes or until toothpick inserted into center comes out clean. Cool completely before frosting.

2. Combine frosting and food coloring in large bowl; mix until desired shade of pink is reached. Place cake on serving plate; frost top and sides. Place strawberries around outer edge of cake and in center. *Makes 20 servings*

Under the Sea

**2 packages (18¼ ounces each) chocolate cake mix. plus
  ingredients to prepare mix
2 containers (16 ounces each) vanilla frosting
  Blue food coloring
  Assorted sea life gummy candies and rock candy**

1. Preheat oven to 350°F. Grease and flour two 13×9-inch cake pans. Prepare cake mixes according to package directions. Bake 32 to 35 minutes or until toothpick inserted into centers comes out clean.

2. Remove cakes from pan; cool completely on wire racks. Combine frosting and food coloring in large bowl; mix until desired shade is reached.

3. Place one cake layer on serving plate. Frost top of cake with frosting. Place second cake on top. Frost top and sides of cake with remaining frosting. Decorate cake as shown in photo or as desired using gummy candies and rock candy. *Makes 24 servings*

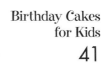

Birthday Cakes
for Kids

41

Pizza Cake

1 package (18¼ ounces) yellow cake mix, plus
    ingredients to prepare mix
1 container (16 ounces) white frosting
    Red food coloring
    Orange round gummy candies
    Sugar-coated sour gummy strips, cut into small pieces
    Purple round sour gummy rings
    White candy-coated licorice strips

1. Preheat oven to 350°F. Grease and flour 12-inch deep dish pizza pan. Prepare cake mix according to package directions. Pour batter into prepared pan. Bake 18 to 25 minutes or until toothpick inserted into center of cake comes out clean. Cool completely before frosting.

2. Place cake on serving plate. Combine frosting and food coloring in medium bowl; mix until desired shade is reached. Frost top of cake to within ¼ inch from edge.

3. Place candies on top to resemble pizza toppings and cheese.

Makes 12 servings

Tropical Parasol Cake

1 package (18¼ ounces) French vanilla cake mix with pudding in the mix, plus ingredients to prepare mix
2 teaspoons coconut extract
2 containers (18 ounces each) white frosting, divided
¼ cup apricot preserves
2 small bananas, sliced ½ inch thick
   Green and blue food coloring
   Shredded coconut
   Yellow decorating sugar
8 parasols

1. Preheat oven to 350°F. Grease and flour two 9-inch round cake pans. Prepare cake mix according to package directions. Add coconut extract to batter; mix well. Divide batter evenly between prepared pans. Bake 22 minutes or until toothpick inserted into centers comes out clean. Cool completely before frosting.

2. Place one cake layer upside down on serving plate. Combine ¾ cup frosting and apricot preserves in medium bowl; mix well. Spread over top of cake. Arrange banana slices over frosting. Top with second cake layer. Combine remaining frosting and green food coloring in large bowl; mix until desired shade is reached. Frost top and side of cake with green frosting.

3. Place coconut in resealable food storage bag; add 8 to 10 drops blue food coloring. Seal bag; shake until coconut is evenly tinted. Press coconut onto cake side. Sprinkle top with yellow sugar. Place open parasols around top of cake.   *Makes 12 servings*

This Way to the Party Zone

2 packages (18¼ ounces each) German chocolate cake mix with pudding in the mix, plus ingredients to prepare mix
½ to ¾ container (16 ounces) lemon frosting
Yellow food coloring
Round gummy candies
Letter-shaped candles or tube frosting
Candy-coated chocolate pieces (optional)

1. Preheat oven to 350°F. Grease 13×9-inch cake pan. Prepare cake mixes according to package directions. Pour all but 2 cups batter into prepared pan; smooth tops. (Reserve remaining batter for another use.) Bake 35 minutes or until toothpick inserted into center comes out clean. Cool completely before frosting.

2. Combine lemon frosting and food coloring in medium bowl; mix until desired shade is reached. Place cake on serving plate. Frost top and sides of cake. Flatten gummy candies with rolling pin, if desired. Make arrow shape with gummy candies as shown in photo. Spell out "Party Zone" inside arrow using candles. Decorate sides of cake with chocolate pieces, if desired.

Makes 20 servings

Swamp Cake

**2 packages (18¼ ounces each) chocolate cake mix, plus
    ingredients to prepare mix**
2 containers (16 ounces each) milk chocolate frosting
1 can (20 ounces) cherry pie filling
**3 chocolate pirouette cookies
    Sugar-coated fruit leathers
    Assorted gumdrops, gummy alligators, gummy frogs
    and Cheddar-flavored fish-shaped crackers**

1. Preheat oven to 350°F. Grease and flour two 13×9-inch cake
pans. Prepare cake mixes according to package directions. Bake
35 to 38 minutes or until toothpick inserted into centers comes out
clean. Cool completely before frosting.

2. Place one cake on serving plate. Frost top of cake. Spread pie
filling to ¼-inch from edge. Place second cake on top. Frost top and
sides of cake with remaining frosting.

3. Place cookies in desired pattern to resemble cypress tree trunks
and limbs. Place pieces of fruit leathers to resemble Spanish moss.
Decorate cake as shown in photo or as desired using candies and
crackers.   *Makes 24 servings*

Birthday Cakes
for Kids

Flower

2 packages (18¼ ounces each) yellow or white cake mix, plus ingredients to prepare mix
2 containers (16 ounces each) vanilla frosting
Food coloring, any two colors
½ cup sweetened shredded coconut
Assorted sprinkles, decorating sugar and candies

1. Preheat oven to 350°F. Grease and flour 8-inch round cake pan. Line 12 large (2¾-inch) and 9 standard (2½-inch) muffin cups with paper baking cups. Prepare 1 package cake of mix according to package directions. Divide batter equally among 12 prepared large muffin cups. Bake 20 to 22 minutes or until toothpick inserted into centers comes out clean. Cool completely before frosting.

2. Prepare remaining package of cake mix according to package directions. Pour half of batter into prepared round pan. Pour remaining batter into 9 standard muffin cups. Bake cake 33 to 36 minutes and cupcakes 18 to 21 minutes or until toothpick inserted into centers comes out clean. Cool completely before frosting.

3. Place round cake on serving platter. Combine half container vanilla frosting and one color of food coloring in small bowl; mix until desired shade is reached. Frost round cake with tinted frosting. Sprinkle coconut over top of cake. Combine remaining frosting and second color of food coloring in large bowl; mix until desired shade is reached. Frost 10 large cupcakes with frosting. Place around cake to resemble flower petals. Decorate cake and cupcakes as desired. Reserve remaining cupcakes for another use.

Makes 18 servings plus 9 extra cupcakes